OJB LANDSCAPE ARCHITECTURE

TABLE OF CONTENTS

FOREWORD

OJB Landscape Architecture has evolved impressively since James Burnett founded it in 1989. Today OJB is one of the foremost landscape architecture practices in the United States, a status the office achieved because of the consistent excellence of its design work. The American Society of Landscape Architects' bestowal of its Firm Award for 2015 on OJB, and Burnett's winning of the Society's Design Medal in 2016 demonstrate how highly he and his associates are regarded by their colleagues in the American landscape architecture profession.

OJB's projects make it clear why such awards and recognition have been forthcoming. OJB's designs are marked by clear spatial structure; a love of plants and a fascination with the ways they affect human perceptions; a remarkable sensitivity to local- and micro-climates, ecologies, and topographies; and a strong sense of how important the social uses of landscape are.

OJB is associated with highly regarded urban design. Klyde Warren Park, which involved constructing a deck atop a downtown Dallas freeway then transforming this platform into a public park and the renewal of the Myriad Botanical Gardens in downtown Oklahoma City both won Urban Open Space Awards from the Urban Land Institute because their beauty functions like a magnet to attract people back to downtown. OJB is associated with highly regarded garden design. At the Brochstein Pavilion at Rice University in Houston and the nine-acre Sunnylands Center and Gardens in Rancho Mirage, OJB made something out of nothing, as the aerial photo of the Sunnylands site shows. The ASLA recognized both with its highest award, the Honor Award for design. OJB is associated with designing places for people. Burbank Studios involved the amazing transformation of leftover space next to a parking lot into a sequence of beguiling outdoor rooms. The Brockman Hall for Physics at Rice University offered OJB a long slot of open-air space underneath a building. Thanks to the office's intervention, it is now a tranquil refuge of greenery, water, and breeze in a hot, humid climate.

OJB Landscape Architecture constructs a poetics of place. This rare skill is what makes its landscapes so charismatic and compelling.

STEPHEN FOX

Stephen Fox is an architectural historian and a Fellow of the Anchorage Foundation of Texas.

PARK / CIVIC

TRANSFORMING CITIES WITH INNOVATIVE OPEN SPACE

OJB's recent work has focused on the aesthetic and economic transformation of American cities through the creation of fascinating and functional public spaces. OJB believes that landscape and open space are critical to rejuvenating and revitalizing cities and can stimulate economic development and urban growth. Cities are increasingly aware of the importance of providing the urban core with well-programmed, beautiful open spaces to attract and retain residents and businesses.

Work in this area contemplates restoring connections between disparate sectors within cities, providing transitional space between residential, cultural, and business districts, and drawing traffic and use through innovative programming initiatives.

Additionally, OJB's urban open space projects have significant environmental benefits, including stormwater runoff interception, carbon emission reduction, and air and noise pollution mitigation. To ensure sustained use and foster vibrant urban communities, spaces are designed with meticulous attention to detail and the needs of the surrounding community in mind.

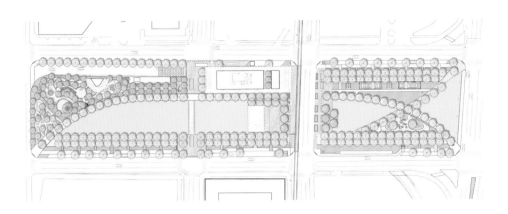

KLYDE WARREN PARK

Klyde Warren Park was created over one of the busiest freeways in Texas. The freeway had severed the city's two largest cultural districts for many years. Restoring the connection has transformed the city by bridging the gap and creating a new heart of downtown. Acting as a common ground for the surrounding museums and businesses, Klyde Warren Park is a vibrant and well-programmed urban park.

Bisected by the existing Olive Street bridge, the park is organized by a sweeping pedestrian promenade that features a continuous canopy of specimen pond cypress. The promenade draws visitors through the park past a botanical garden, a children's garden with an interactive water feature, a reading room, and an event lawn. A large public plaza adjacent to Olive Street connects the restaurant terrace, the performance pavilion, and the casual take-out pavilion to the street and features an interactive fountain feature.

The park has measurably decreased noise and air pollution in the area and increased activity for businesses and cultural institutions. Moreover, real estate and property values surrounding the park have seen a steady increase since the start of construction. Klyde Warren Park has gracefully reconnected the city, and has become an integral and endeared open space in Downtown Dallas.

Location: Dallas, TX
Client: Woodall Rodgers Park Foundation
Team: Jacobs Engineering Group, Thomas Phifer and Partners, Biederman Redevelopment Ventures,
           Endres Ware, Fluidity Design Consultants, Focus Lighting
Awards: Urban Land Institute (ULI) Urban Open Space Award
           ASLA Southern California Design Award
           Texas Society of Architects Honor Award
           Federal Highway Administration Environmental Excellence Award
           D-Magazine - Best Community Impact

MYRIAD BOTANICAL GARDENS

A key component in Oklahoma City's Project 180 public works program, the renovation of Myriad Botanical Gardens has transformed 15 quiet, underutilized acres of open space into a highly programmed urban park and the center of downtown public life. Two decades after its original opening, the park's Crystal Bridge Conservatory, lake, and gardens were popular for portrait photography; but limited accessibility, a lack of programming, and a public perception that the garden was unsafe discouraged repeat visits. OJB worked with a broad coalition of public and private stakeholders to re-envision the park as a vibrant and iconic setting for the city's civic and cultural events.

The framework of the park evolved to preserve over 300 high-value specimen trees and to direct on-site stormwater to the renovated central lake, where it supplements irrigation. Permeable and inviting along its edges, the Garden draws visitors onto a tree-lined promenade that loops through botanical plantings around the lake's upper rim. Quiet, shaded berms to the northwest overlook the 28,000-SF Great Lawn and a sculptural bandshell by Gensler's David Epstein. Along Hudson Avenue to the west, a grove of sycamore trees buffers the street while providing flexible garden space to support Oklahoma City's annual Festival of the Arts. To the south, an interactive water feature marks the entry to a children's garden that balances active play with natural learning. A dog park, a fountain plaza, and a restaurant with outdoor dining enliven the eastern portion of the site.

Extensive programming by the Myriad Garden Foundation utilizes the park's garden rooms year-round for a variety of purposes including concerts, plays, weddings, galas, and sports and fitness events. Since its 2011 re-opening, the park has welcomed more than a million visitors annually and catalyzed downtown economic development, earning it a ULI Urban Open Space Award.

Location: Oklahoma City, OK
Client: The City of Oklahoma City, Myriad Gardens Foundation
Team: Gensler, Fluidity Design Consultants, Endres Ware, Fisher Marantz Stone Partners, Pacific Aquascape, Murase Associates, Alvine Engineering, Cardinal Engineering, Thornton Tomasetti, Frankfurt-Short-Bruza Associates, Robert Birchell and Associates, Sweeney & Associates, Dyal and Partners, Mary Irish, Mike Schnelle
Awards: Urban Land Institute (ULI) Urban Open Space Award
ASLA San Diego Merit Award

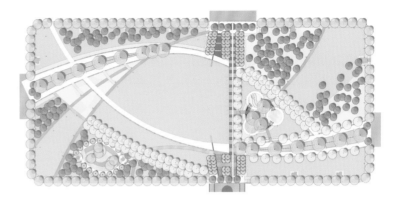

THE PARK AT LAKESHORE EAST

The Park at Lakeshore East is a 5.3-acre urban park that is the central amenity of the 28-acre Lakeshore East development in Chicago's Inner Loop. Overlooking the confluence of the Chicago River and Lake Michigan, Lakeshore East is a $4B redevelopment that includes 4,950 residential units, 1,500 hotel rooms, 2.2 million GSF of commercial space, 770,000 SF of retail space and an elementary school.

Two sweeping promenades serve as the primary circulation across the site, and each features a series of fountain basins, seating areas, and ornamental gardens. An extension of Field Street's axis, the Grand Stair offers a commanding view of the park and accommodates the 25' grade differential created by Chicago's three-tiered transit system. Additional amenities include a children's garden, dog park, and event lawn.

Location: Chicago, IL
Client: Lakeshore East, City of Chicago, Magellan Development Group
Team: Skidmore, Owings & Merrill, Site Design Group
Awards: AIA Excellence in Regional and Urban Design
                FIABCI Prix d'Excellence Award
                ASLA Texas Chapter Merit Award
                Friends of Downtown Chicago Best New Open Space
                Chicago Magazine - Best New Park
                Builder Magazine - Builder's Choice

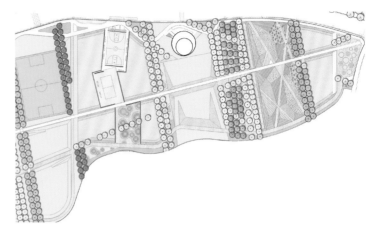

PLAYA VISTA CENTRAL PARK

Located on the former site of Howard Hughes' aircraft facility, Playa Vista Central Park is part of the last entitled development sites remaining in the Los Angeles area. Conceived as a public art installation, the park is organized into a series of distinct landscape experiences unified by a central spine and linear bands of specimen trees.

Together with Michael Maltzan Architects, OJB designed a central nine-acre park consisting of sports courts, playground, soccer field, botanical gardens, water features, and a bandshell. The park serves as the social hub for the campus. Each parcel has park-front access or direct views to the central green, providing a strong relationship between architecture and landscape. Richly landscaped courts and roof gardens are integrated into the proposed buildings and existing historic edifices providing tenants with easy access to the famed outdoor environment of Southern California.

Marked with signature benches and earth forms, the entry plaza greets visitors to the park before leading them into a berm garden that features bold installations of regionally-appropriate plant material. Central to the park is a function lawn and performance pavilion surrounded by bosques of shade trees. Colorful sports courts and an imaginative children's garden seem to float in the middle of a nearby lake and provide a unique identity to the park.

Location: Los Angeles, CA
Client: Playa Vista Capital
Team: Michael Maltzan Architecture, Psomas, Isenberg & Associates, Biesek Design, HLB Lighting
           Design, Arup, Sweeney & Associates, West Coast Design Group, Pacific Aquascape,
           Terra-Petra, Group Delta Consultants, Community Arts Resources

PROJECT 180 STREETSCAPE

OJB worked with the City of Oklahoma City to renovate the streetscape in the downtown area. Project 180 presented the opportunity to revitalize and completely renew the urban core of Oklahoma City. The streetscape and street improvements encompass more than 180 acres of the Central Business District, including the alignments of 17 streets. Nearly eight miles of streets were updated with new intersections, pavement, site amenities, continuous street trees, and abundant on-street parking. OJB directed the efforts of a large subconsultant team to narrow downtown streets, create habitable street environments, and establish streetscape design standards.

Location: Oklahoma City, OK
Client: The City of Oklahoma City
Team: Murase Associates, Speck & Associates, Howard-Fairbairn
           Site Design, Carter Design Group, CLS and Associates,
           Robert Lewis & Associates, Cardinal Engineering, Coon Engineering,
           Darr & Collins Consulting Engineers, Guernsey, Legacy Engineering,
           Lemke Land Surveying, MacArthur Associated Consultants,
           Myers Engineering, Smith Roberts Baldischwiler, Tetra Tech,
           Traffic Engineering Consultants, White Engineering Associates,
           LIFANG International

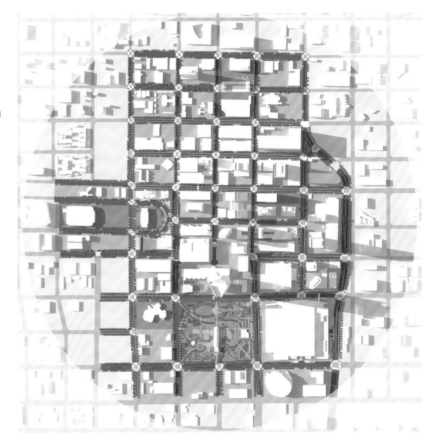

LEBAUER PARK

In 2013, the estate of Carolyn and Maurice LeBauer gifted the Community Foundation of Greater Greensboro with a bequest to create a new urban park for "the benefit and enjoyment of the general population of Greensboro, particularly children and their families."

Located on a 3.3-acre site in the heart of downtown Greensboro, the park's final implementation will realign key downtown streets to encourage a stronger relationship with the upcoming Steven Tanger Performing Arts Center and will become the heart of a new cultural arts district.

The park is organized around a concert lawn and performance pavilion that will be crowned with a permanent installation from renowned Boston-based artist Janet Echelman. The actively programmed park will also include a significant children's garden and interactive water feature, dog park, reading room, games area, a croquet lawn, and putting green. It is anticipated the park will be financially self-sustaining. In addition to including several food and beverage kiosks, it will also accommodate the wide range of festivals and other civic-scale events from the greater Greensboro area.

Location: Greensboro, NC
Client: Community Foundation of Greater Greensboro
Team: Moser Mayer Phoenix Associates, Frank Harmon Architect, Fountain Source, Focus Lighting
           Light Defines Form, Westcott, Small and Associates, Engineered Concepts, Chip Callaway &
           Associates, Arup, RSM Design, Boulton Creative, Pine & Swallow Environmental,
           Biederman Redevelopment Ventures

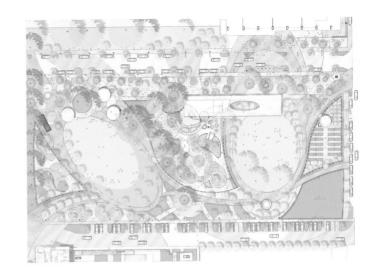

LEVY PARK

Levy Park is a highly programmed 5.9-acre urban park located within the residential development project in the Upper Kirby District of Houston. The Upper Kirby Redevelopment Authority, a public-private partnership, hired OJB to design a world-class urban park.

Programming for the park will include a performance pavilion, two large event lawns, a community garden, several water features, and a dog park to ensure that the gardens offer something for everyone. A generous promenade circling the park will connect a games area, play berms, decomposed granite seating courts, and a food kiosk. Several mixed-use residential and office buildings sit across the street and are united with the park by the surrounding renovated streetscapes. At the heart of the park is a winding children's garden, which among its playful fountains and tree houses, will sit several 40-70-year-old legacy live oak trees that were relocated on-site.

Location: Houston, TX
Client: The Upper Kirby Redevelopment Authority
Team: Natalye Appel + Associates, Ward, Getz & Associates, Matrix Structural Engineers,
           WYLIE Consulting Engineers, Fountain Source, Biederman Redevelopment Ventures,
           4b Technology, Minor Design

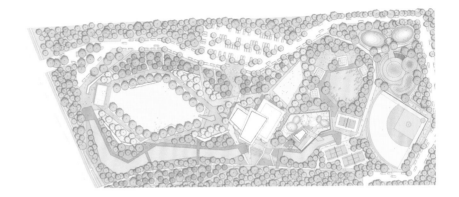

VETERANS MEMORIAL PARK

Commemorating our veterans and their families with memorials has always been an American tradition. However, a new approach to celebrating our soldiers and their dedication to our country can have a profound effect throughout the community. Veterans Park can provide a new park model that serves as a testament to all the brave men and women who have sacrificed their lives for the United States of America.

Memorials customarily honor those service people who have passed, but it is equally important that we recognize our present-day soldiers as well. Veterans Park provides a space that celebrates our country's military history, unifies our armed forces, and creates a memorable park experience to be shared by all.

Veterans Park is 21.5 acres of green space that accommodates all users. Upon arrival, commemorative walls focus on telling stories of our country's military history. The northern part of the park features passive walks throughout while the southern side offers a contrasting active experience with the children's playground, activity lawn, and recreation fields. The northern and southern portions of the park are linked by a boardwalk and an interpretative wetland terrace for a unique pedestrian experience. At the heart of the park rests the visitor's center that serves as the organizing body for all park events.

Beginning at the northern entrance to the park, flags for our armed forces welcome visitors. This entry plaza begins to engage park visitors with the strong lines of the commemorative walls that cut through the ground plane and echo a strong code of discipline and order. Just beyond the first commemorative wall in the entry plaza sits a multi-use event pavilion. Further in, pedestrian walks and resilient allées of signature live oaks highlight a grand open space for celebration along the one-acre parade field.

Location: Houston, TX
Client: City of Houston

NORTH HOUSTON BIKE PARK

North Houston Bike Park encompasses more than 22 acres, centrally located between Downtown Houston, The Woodlands, and Kingwood, Texas. The Greater Greenspoint Redevelopment Authority hired OJB to design this one-of-a-kind, world-class bike park following the completion of the ten-acre North Houston Skate Park which lies directly to the north. The creation of this area has already provided a benefit to the local community and impacted development in the neighboring region.

The focus for the North Houston Bike Park is to provide something for everybody, whether it's novice or expert riders, visitors, or spectators. Programming for the park will include a BMX track, a welcome center, 25,000 SF of concrete bike bowls, a performance pavilion with large event lawn, an urban riding plaza, large and small pump tracks, a tot track, a dirt jumps track, and off-road trails with break-out areas for various skill work.

OJB has incorporated sustainable elements into the design, and the park is being built to be space-efficient. The starting ramp sits atop the park's 2,500-SF Welcome Center. Another unique element provided to visitors entering from the north is the pedestrian bridge which is situated on top of rideable planters and allows visitors to traverse the bike bowls. Visitors can take advantage of this distinctive vantage point with birds-eye views of the riders below as well as tree-top sightlines extending to the south end of the park.

Promenades run the length of the park, framing the event lawn and creating a variety of pedestrian gathering spaces. Bike activity happens to the east and west of the promenades ensuring an active experience for all visitors.

Location: Houston, TX
Client: The Greater Greenspoint Redevelopment Authority
Team: Endrestudio, Walter P. Moore and Associates, Wylie Consulting Engineers, Stantec,
           SITE Design Group, Minor Design, Carter Design Group, Jones | Carter

CULTURAL

CELEBRATING LEGACY THROUGH DESIGN

Cultural landscapes become institutions within their communities, inspiring emotions and memories that resonate with visitors. OJB's cultural landscapes strive to embrace the essence of a particular place. Whether an inviting entry or a hidden oasis, the landscape serves to capture a moment. Guests become captivated by their surroundings, mapping a relationship with the site that enlightens them to the identity of the space.

Attention to consciously designed experiences strengthens the connection of visitor to site and site to structure. Guests are invited to explore the grounds and associate with the projected story as it's told through an ensemble of orchestrated moments.

SUNNYLANDS CENTER AND GARDENS

Pioneering a new ecological aesthetic for arid landscapes in the southwest, Sunnylands Center & Gardens is a nine-acre desert jewel amid Rancho Mirage's conventional, thirsty sprawl. The new Interpretive Center and Botanical Gardens celebrate the cultural legacy of publisher, diplomat, and philanthropist Walter Annenberg and his wife Lenore, whose adjacent 200-acre estate has long been a retreat for U.S. Presidents, foreign dignitaries, and celebrities. Working closely with Mrs. Annenberg, OJB created a collection of museum-quality garden spaces that invite discovery and reflection.

Organic and free-flowing at the edges of the site, the lines of hardscape surfaces and planting beds take on a geometric precision adjacent to the Center. Located past a gracious entry drive and formal auto court, Frederick Fisher and Partners' 15,000-SF LEED Gold-rated building houses exhibition space, a café, a theater, and a gift shop. The Center's western windows frame a breathtaking view over an event terrace and lawn to the 10,000-foot-high San Jacinto Mountains beyond. To the right and left of the terrace, twin reflecting basins mirror the expansive desert sky, lower the ambient temperature, and fill the area with the relaxing sound of water. More than 1.25 miles of walking trails lead visitors past the circular event lawn, beneath flowering palo verde desert trees, to a labyrinth garden, a performance circle, and interpretive displays of native plants.

The planting design features 53,000 hand-picked specimens from over 50 arid-landscape plant species chosen for their sculptural character, seasonal interest, and wildlife habitat value. Cutting-edge water efficiency measures throughout the site allow the garden to thrive using only 20% of its water allocation from the Coachella Valley Water District.

Location: Rancho Mirage, CA
Client: Annenberg Foundation Trust
Team: Frederick Fisher and Partners, CMS Collaborative, HLB Lighting Design, Hillmann & Carr, MSA Consulting, Litwak Group
Awards: ASLA National Design Award
ASLA San Diego Design Award
Architectural Foundation of Los Angeles (AFLA) Design Award

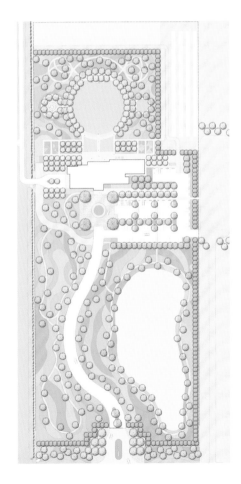

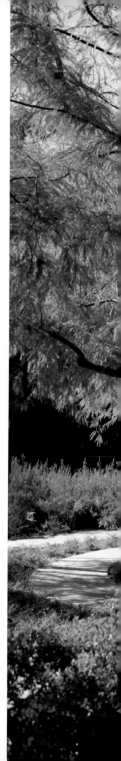

ASIA SOCIETY TEXAS CENTER

Located on a 1.5-acre parcel in Houston's Museum District, the 38,000-SF Asia Society Texas Center is sited to take advantage of the distant Houston skyline. The Center uses Arts and Cultural programming to promote the bonds of cultural understanding within the greater Houston community.

Visitors are welcomed by a landscape that adheres to a thoughtfully executed minimalist ethic. The front yard includes a simple plane of ground cover and heritage oaks that frame views to the main entry and serves as a venue for special events. At the rear of the building, a grove of bald cypress forms a vertical hedge that holds the views to the second level Stone Garden.

A series of three individual gardens are located on the second level of the building. The Water Garden features a skin of water that reflects shadows from two heritage oaks and the Houston skyline. The Stone Garden is a contemporary expanse of gravel and vertical bamboo that serves as a backdrop to rotating pieces of sculpture at the Center. The Sculpture Garden includes a sloped carpet of ground cover with stone sculptures carefully placed in the composition.

Location: Houston, TX
Client: Asia Society Texas Center
Team: Taniguchi and Associates, Kendall/Heaton Associates, GBA Architecture, Ingenium, CHPA Consulting Engineers, Walter P. Moore, Fisher Marantz Stone, Waterscape Consulting, Shen Milsom & Wilke, Minor Design

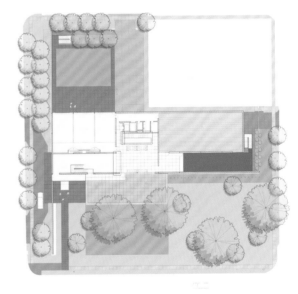

WORKPLACE

RE-ENVISIONING THE COLLABORATIVE WORKSPACE

In an effort to nurture a fulfilled and productive workforce, many employers are accommodating personnel with the establishment of exterior amenity spaces that provide both active and passive recreation. Areas offering moments of quiet reflection and respite, intermixed with communal, lively spaces, deliver a combination sought after by today's talented workforce.

OJB specializes in developing a creative environment that inspires the imagination and nourishes creativity. From company sponsored events to impromptu team meetings, individuals discover a balance amid the alluring landscape. The inviting exterior spaces are framed with regionally appropriate plant palettes and are designed with acute attention to current sustainability practices.

PRIVATE CAMPUS

On this 94-acre campus, carefully detailed outdoor spaces artfully manage the site's stormwater and create a serene setting for seven buildings, housing administrative offices, research facilities, a cafeteria, a childcare center, and a wellness center. This design renovation consolidates disparate facilities from across the Houston metropolitan area into a new-world headquarters on the site of an existing manufacturing and shipping facility. OJB worked closely with the architect to ensure that the overall design was environmentally responsible, preserved the site's unique character, and created a home for the many programmatic needs of the people working there.

New structures are located towards the interior of the site, preserving forest canopy along the perimeter and insulating personnel from manufacturing operations. Large interior stands of trees were preserved and more than 500 new trees were planted to give scale, shade, and separation on this very large site. The buildings are organized around a central lake that serves as amenity and focal point for the campus while managing its runoff. Adjacent to the lake, wetland systems planted extensively with native vegetation provide additional detention and create wildlife habitat.

Artfully arranged around the buildings, waterways, and islands, a series of compatible outdoor use areas – gravel terraces, hardwood decks, trellis-shaded walkways – invite users out into the landscape to relax, play, and socialize. Throughout the campus, the sweeping elliptical lines of the lake are echoed in the design of water features, walkways, decks, and planting beds.

Location: Houston, TX
Client: Confidential
Team: Gensler, Ward, Getz & Associates, Haynes Whaley Associates,
  Wylie Consulting Engineers
Awards: ASLA Texas Chapter Merit Award

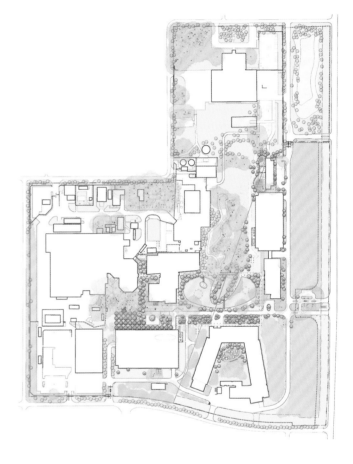

LA JOLLA COMMONS

Located in the University Town Center district of San Diego, La Jolla Commons is an 18-acre, three-phase office and hotel development organized around a two-acre green space. Hines Interests engaged OJB to develop the central garden in conjunction with the phase two tower, a 13-story, 300,000-SF Class A commercial office tower and one of the largest Net Zero buildings in the United States. Working with notable Los Angeles architect Paul Danna, OJB created a campus with a relaxed Southern California atmosphere and resort-style amenities.

Sweeping pedestrian promenades define the function lawn and organize circulation between the two office towers, the expanded on-site parking structure, and an additional parking structure across Executive Drive. A basketball court and putting green are located at the perimeter of the site, while interior amenities include a dining terrace, a gravel court with a fire feature and lounge chairs, and a shaded plaza with a reflecting basin and movable furniture.

The landscape design contributes to the Net Zero certification by employing Low Impact Design strategies. Site grading directs runoff from the curbless entry drive and parking areas into a linear bioswale that runs the length of the park. The planting design incorporates sweeping masses of jewel-toned succulents and drought-tolerant grasses appropriate to the Southern California climate.

Location: La Jolla, CA
Client: Hines, JP Morgan Asset Management
Team: AECOM, Leppert Engineering, Nabih Youseff Associates, WSP Flack + Kurtz
HMA Consulting
Awards: ASLA San Diego Design Award

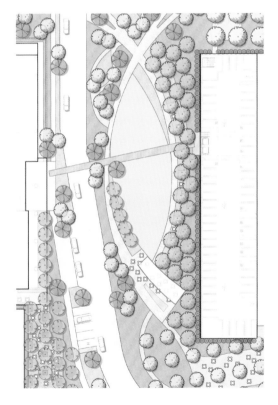

THE CAMPUS AT PLAYA VISTA

Developed as a component of the 64-acre Playa Vista master plan, this 6.5-acre office development features structured parking and four separate buildings totaling 325,000 SF of Class A office space. Richly detailed courtyards utilize combinations of paving materials and drought-tolerant plants to create a unique mood and identity for each building entry.

Third-floor terraces built over the garage deck are shared by the building tenants and feature modest event lawns, seating areas, ornamental planting, and sweeping panoramas of the Santa Monica mountains to Downtown Los Angeles. Each building also features an extensive green roof planted with regionally-appropriate plant materials and a small private terrace to minimize the impact of thermal heat gain and stormwater runoff.

Location: Los Angeles, CA
Client: Playa Vista Capital Management, Tishman Speyer
Team: Gensler, HLB Lighting Design, Psomas, Environmental International Corporation

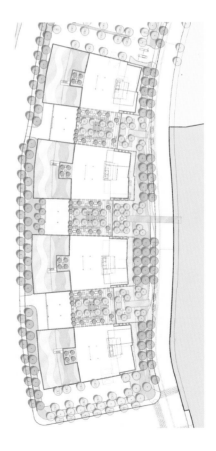

THE FAIRWAY BUILDING AT BURBANK STUDIOS

Burbank Studios is a legacy Hollywood broadcasting center and home of the former NBC Studios. Master planned by Gehry Partners, Worthe Real Estate Group redeveloped the 1920's and 50's era studios into a 35-acre state-of-the-art film and TV broadcast facility.

Largely an industrial film production center, OJB has re-imagined the face of The Fairway Building, the largest and most central studio building on-site, to include a 630-foot by 40-foot linear courtyard and garden workspace.

The complete east face of The Fairway Building, formerly a loading dock, has been broken into eight programmed terraces which house games, seating and dining areas, micro-lawns, and collaborative seating spaces. The historic awnings which sit atop the plinth loading dock, have been selectively peeled pack to reveal the existing canopy frame structure. Trees sit on structure and at grade to lead guests and tenants into the space, while a vertical vine cable system supports greenscreens to offer a semi-transparent enclosure within the courtyard. A series of five water features stretching the length of the site provide visual interest and cool the space, while vibrant ornamental planting counters and complements the industrial architecture and creates a welcome respite from the harder surroundings.

The courtyards serve as a breakout and collaboration space for the three tenants within the building and act as a social and visual hub. The Fairway Building set the bar for the inaugural phase of Burbank Studios' redevelopment.

Location: Burbank, CA
Client: Worthe Real Estate Group
Team: ARC, Candela, Sweeney & Associates, Fountain Source,
           HLB Lighting Design, Sukow Engineering

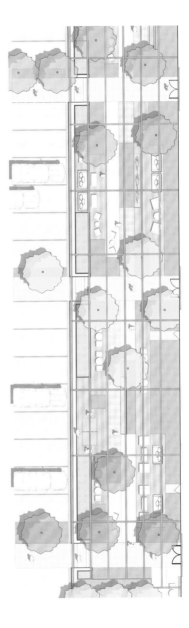

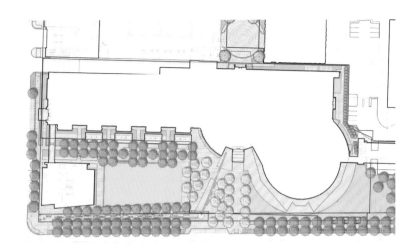

DEVON ENERGY WORLD HEADQUARTERS

This 2.25-acre space is a simple yet elegant composition of lawn, shade trees, and special water features, that acts as a foreground for the podium, Winter Garden, and tower. A cascading wall of water enhances the entry experience and buffers the park from the activity of the plaza and street.

Organized around a living pool teeming with aquatic life, the informal dining terrace overlooks a public green that accommodates 1,500-2,000 people during special events. Along the north edge of the lawn, rich plantings and a series of overflowing fountain features insulate private courtyards from the activity of the park. At the western edge of the park, an elegant pavilion rises from a skin of water and provides a space for special events as well as the activities of the everyday lunch crowd.

Location: Oklahoma City, OK
Client: Devon Energy
Team: Pickard Chilton, Kendall/Heaton Associates, Quentin Thomas Associates, Murase Associates,
               Fluidity Design Consultants, Gensler, Thornton Thomasetti, Cosentini Associates,
               Smith Roberts Baldischwiler, HMA Consulting
Awards   Urban Land Institute (ULI) Global Award for Excellence

PARTNERS HEALTHCARE ADMINISTRATIVE CAMPUS

Partners HealthCare System is Massachusetts' largest private employer, hospital network, and physician's organization. Partners will consolidate administrative operations from 14 sites in the eastern part of the state and move 4,500 non-hospital employees into a new 700,000-SF office building scheduled to open at Somerville's massive Assembly Row development in late 2016.

Assembly Row, a mixed-use project being developed by Federal Realty Investment Trust, is planned as a 45-acre redevelopment of former industrial property. Located along the Mystic River in what is now Somerville's Assembly Square, the historic site once housed a Ford Motor Co. factory.

The project will be focused around a 2.5-acre open space which will include a variety of amenities for Partners' users and the general public. Looking to become a benchmark for sustainable strategies in the region, the campus will employ best management practices for water conservation, the use of native and adaptive plant materials, and local/regional building materials throughout the site.

Location: Somerville, MA
Client: Partners HealthCare System
Team: Gensler, Vanasse Hangen Brustlin, BuroHappold Engineering, Haley & Aldrich, HLB Lighting Design, Ryan Associates

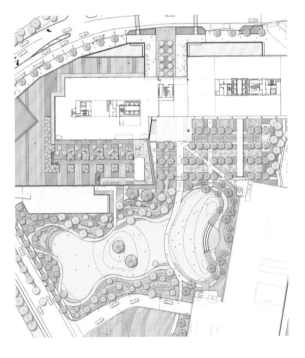

CONOCOPHILLIPS WORLD HEADQUARTERS

The renovation of this corporate campus created a new core of office, medical, fitness, and public space on the 62-acre project site. Originally developed as a passive suburban landscape, the new design integrates a variety of programmed areas throughout the campus.

Sited to preserve existing specimen live oaks, the new campus entry features a formal auto court and a series of cascading water features. Smaller garden courtyards lead to the central Commons, which features a number of private dining terraces and an event lawn that accommodates 1,000 people. To promote employee wellness, the site also features a two-mile jogging path and a two-thirds regulation size soccer field.

Client: ConocoPhillips
Team: Pickard Chilton Architects, Kendall/Heaton Associates, PDR Corporation,
             Haynes Whaley Associates, I.A. Naman + Associates, Walter P. Moore
Awards: ASLA Texas Design Award

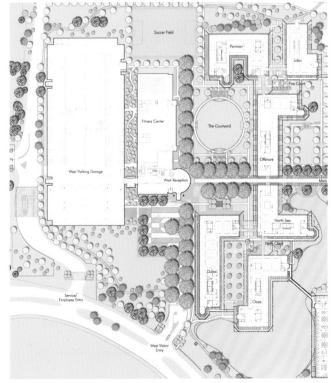

WELLNESS AND HOSPITALITY

CULTIVATING RESTORATIVE EXPERIENCES

Creating unique lifestyle experiences for guests is at the forefront of expectations within the present-day hospitality and wellness industry. OJB possesses a thorough understanding of the market and instills an integrated vision and foresight into the creation of uniquely identifiable spaces. In turn, these spaces become opportunities for a multitude of flexible amenities that elicit an assortment of experiences.

A harmonious interchange amongst the materials palette, in conjunction with modern amenities, such as external WiFi, produces the anticipated moments sought after by visitors. While guests relax amidst the intuitively designed experiences, clients appreciate the return on investment of the judiciously programmed site.

THE JW MARRIOTT

The JW Marriott Austin is an upscale boutique hotel in downtown Austin. Situated on an open fifth level terrace, a deck featuring a pool and amenities offers guests multiple options for outdoor activity.

Providing the backdrop for the deck is a series of green wall columns, planted with vines, along the south facing façade of the building. Private cabana rooms are nestled within the columns, while chaise lounges offer more social seating out on the open deck. The various lounging areas are located around the pool and outdoor bar. Raised and flush planters, canopy trees, and an outdoor fire pit all provide interest for users. Open, flexible-use space is available via an artificial turf-lawn function space on the western side of the deck.

The design of the deck spaces is accentuated by attention to details and materials, such as the use of plants with interesting textures, cool paving, and attractive landscape lighting. The amenity deck is a flagship feature of the JW Marriott Austin Hotel.

Location: Austin, TX
Client: White Lodging
Team: HKS, Counsilman-Hunsaker, Magnusson Klemencic Associates, Blum Consulting Engineers,
           MCLA, Sweeney & Associates, Bury

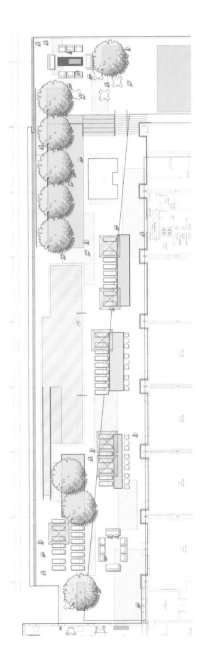

HALL WINES

A sensitive blend of modernism and tradition, the new and renovated facilities and gardens at Craig and Kathryn Hall's Napa Valley winery expand their sizable production capability and provide a world-class hospitality destination for their growing brand. OJB worked with the Halls to create a five-acre garden that invites exploration of this beautiful working landscape, accommodates the winery's many special events, and provides a refined setting for the significant sculpture collection.

A renovated entry along Highway 29 employs specimen shade trees, exuberant perennial plantings, and a signature sculpture to draw visitors through the working organic vineyards to a new auto court organized around a magnificent preserved valley oak. A straight sightline connects this tree with the main entry to the new Visitor Center. Located along this walk, an arrival court beneath a grove of shade trees serves as a gathering area for winery tours.

Signum Architecture's state-of-the-art, 30,000-SF Visitor Center features the Hall's extensive collection of modern art throughout reception areas, public and private tasting rooms, and a ground level demonstration kitchen that opens onto a dining and event terrace.

The winery hosts music, culinary and cultural events on a 6,500-SF Great Lawn adjacent to the renovated Peterson-Bergfeld historic building. At the vineyards' edge, a gravel terrace with a long granite reflection basin, umbrellas, and lounge chairs affords spectacular views of the Mayacamas Mountains. Low limestone walls divide the northern gardens into discrete rooms dedicated to cut flower production, an organic kitchen garden, and the Olive Grove which doubles as a rotating gallery for art installations.

Location: St. Helena
Client: HALL Wines
Team: Signum Architecture, Summit Engineering, HLB Lighting Design, Fluidity Design Consultants, NICOLEHOLLIS, Jesús Moroles, Sweeney and Associates

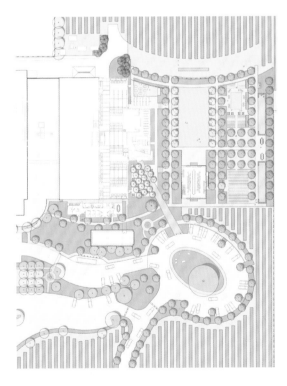

OMEGA AT THE CROSSINGS

Located on 210 acres of fragile land in the Texas Hill Country, The Crossings is a destination spa and wellness center overlooking beautiful Lake Travis. With 70 guest rooms distributed across eight lodges, The Crossings campus also features a carriage house, welcome center, sanctuary, dining hall, and numerous landscape amenities.

Incorporating green design elements was a high client priority. OJB limited pervious paving across the site to maximize the amount of rainfall that percolates through to the Edwards Aquifer. Both rainwater and effluent are harvested on-site to feed the irrigation system, and most materials on the site are locally sourced. With the exception of the two highly manicured areas near the Visitor Center, the site is planted extensively with native or drought-tolerant material.

Client: Joyce & Ken Beck, Omega Institute
Team: Hatch Partnership Architects
Awards: ASLA Texas Chapter Merit Award

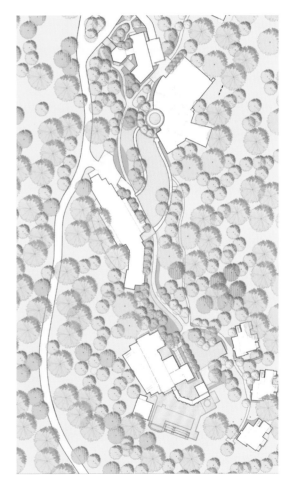

THE CHRIST HOSPITAL

The Christ Hospital landscape master plan is designed to create a warm and inviting atmosphere for patients, visitors, and staff. Reflecting the cultural personality of Cincinnati and the rich historical signature of the Mt. Auburn neighborhood, the landscape respects and pays homage to the past while celebrating the future.

A series of landscaped courts dedicated to a wide array of departments and users provides outlets for gathering, waiting, reflecting, and healing. Implementing cutting-edge sustainability practices, an optimized campus experience, and enhanced accessibility and circulation all contribute to the ultimate success of the design. By encouraging expansion and responsible growth, the landscape master plan creates a benchmark for the healthcare experience.

Location: Cincinnati, OH
Client: The Christ Hospital
Team: Skidmore, Owings and Merrill, Fosdick & Hilmer, Champlin Architects,
           THP Limited, Schuler Shook

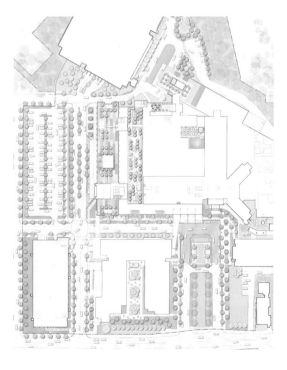

LIVE
WORK
PLAY

ARTFULLY BLENDING
VARIED ENVIRONMENTS

Mixed-use projects have been known to instill a sense of place, spur vitality, and rejuvenate communities. Focused development encourages high-quality design and offers a spectrum of amenities, all within reach. By intelligently utilizing a smaller footprint, mixed-use projects promote the protection of outlying areas and environmentally sensitive resources while activating the street level and enlivening often underutilized areas.

OJB leverages extensive experience in designing for mixed-use spaces that successfully marry different environments. Varied programming attracts a diverse demographic by offering something for everyone, whether they are looking to live, work, or play. As populations grow and space decreases, multipurpose projects are increasingly viewed as viable solutions, harmoniously blending the best of retail, hospitality, office, recreation, and entertainment.

METROPOLIS

Situated on the edge of Downtown Los Angeles, blocks from the Staples Center, the Metropolis Towers are a mixed-use complex consisting of 1,250 luxury residential units with two floors of high-end retail along the street. Located over the parking garage and between the two towers is a 60,000-SF amenity deck with dramatic views of downtown and Hollywood Hills.

This California Modern inspired amenity deck features a lap pool, spa area, event pavilion, activity lawns, dog park, and children's play area, all situated in a richly landscaped garden. Event terraces are located midway at each of the towers and feature outdoor kitchens, gathering areas, a small event lawn, and rich ornamental planting.

Location:	Los Angeles, CA
Team:	Harley Ellis Devereaux, Breen Engineering, Saiful Bouquet,
	CD+M Lighting Design Group, Aquatic Design Group, HLB Lighting
Renderings:	NeoScape

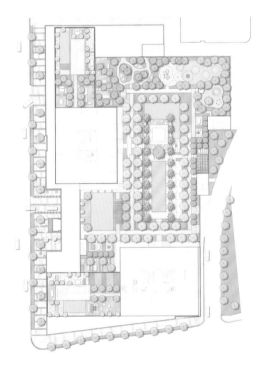

CITYCENTRE HOUSTON

CityCentre Houston is a 47-acre, mixed-use development where exceptional public spaces and streetscapes integrate the many offerings - offices, residences, hotels, restaurants, retail, conference, fitness, cinema, and structured parking - into a cohesive whole. When the Midway Development Group purchased a failing shopping mall on 37 acres at the intersection of two major Houston highways (two more parcels acquired for later phases added ten additional acres), they engaged OJB to guide and implement their vision for a complete, walkable urban destination.

The heart of CityCentre is the public plaza enclosed by the 13-story Hotel Sorella to the west, by one and two-story restaurant and retail buildings to the north and south, and by the five-story CityCentre One office building to the east of Town and Country Boulevard. An intimate event lawn, water and fire features, and outdoor seating for ground-level restaurants extend the hospitality atmosphere of the hotel out into the landscape, making it ideal for a variety of programmed and spontaneous outdoor activities. The plaza's paving pattern flows into and across the boulevard to CityCentre One. The design captures additional capacity for special events when the street is closed to automobile traffic.

Throughout the site, carefully detailed paving patterns, planting islands, curbs, and grade changes calm traffic and prioritize pedestrian movement. This inviting and well-used series of outdoor spaces and streetscapes is integral to the success of CityCentre, which was featured in an Urban Land Institute case study and is becoming a benchmark for mixed-use urban developments.

Location: Houston, TX
Client: Midway Companies
Team: Gensler, Valencia, Walter P. Moore, Thomson Company, Haynes Whaley Associates
Awards: ASLA Texas Chapter Honor Award
           Urban Land Institute (ULI) Houston Development of Distinction Award

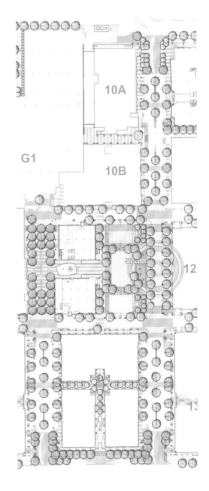

SPRINGWOODS VILLAGE CITYPLACE PARK

CityPlace is a 60-acre mixed-use urban district featuring heavy office, retail, and residential components. The Town Center is designed around the Plaza, which features restaurants, a water feature, and a flexible green space.

Located adjacent to the Town Center and Plaza, CityPlace Lake's thoughtfully planned landscape design consists of a series of eight ponds, waterfalls, open activity areas, multi-use trails, and boardwalks, which provide many opportunities for visitors and residents alike. Springwoods CityPlace Lake is the first drainage corridor/park system from Interstate 45 and acts as one of three of the community's drainage corridor systems.

OJB designed the community master plan as well as the landscape for the Town Center and CityPlace Lake.

Location: Springwoods, TX
Client: Coventry Development Corporation

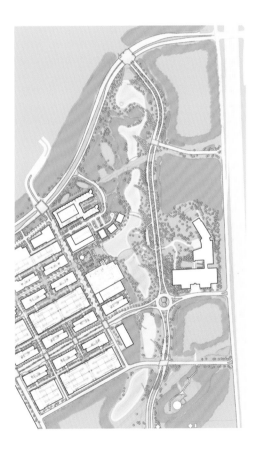

ARBOLEDA

Envisioned as a mixed-use development, Arboleda will be a premier model for sustainable development in San Pedro Garza Garcia, which serves as an important corporate center in Monterrey, Mexico. The master plan will create a new urban center on a 26-acre site next to the Campestre Golf Club with dramatic views of the Sierra Madre Mountains.

At the core of the project, the leaf shaped park serves as a significant outdoor area, providing a distinct open space and a rich experience for the public and residents. The development will include a vibrant commercial zone and a secure, private residential area, both organized around a central park.

Arboleda offers a diverse variety of site programming. Residents will live in three towers and smaller scaled villas in the residential area and two midrise apartment buildings in the commercial district. This lively, walkable district for business and entertainment will also include office towers, office gardens, restaurants, stores, café bistro, a performance pavilion, a hotel, and a cultural center. The clubhouse will link the commercial and residential zones and will be an amenity for all.

Highlighting the projects' emphasis on sustainable design, it will be compliant with LEED for Neighborhood Development, a system of design which integrates the principles of smart growth, urbanism, and green building.

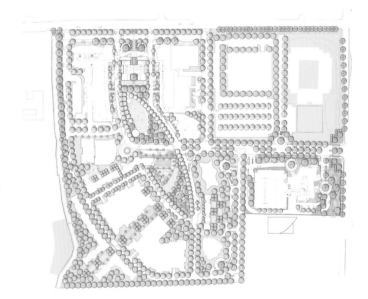

Location: Monterrey, Mexico
Client: One Development Group
Team: Pelli Clarke Pelli Architects, HKS, KMD Architects, JSa Arquitectura,
            RDLP Arquitectos, Fountain Source, HWA Parking, Quentin Thomas Associates,
            Environmental Design

WESTFIELD CENTURY CITY

Westfield Century City is an upgrade to the existing outdoor mall in the heart of Century City in Los Angeles. The re-imagined experience will feature 422,000 SF of new retail space punctuated by 70 new high-fashion street-side boutiques for a total of 220 of the world's most prestigious shops and restaurants.

Eight acres of outdoor space, including a new central courtyard plaza will lead visitors through open-air cafés and plazas housing world-class restaurants, while several central events and entertainment spaces will activate the site day and night.

Westfield Century City's transformation will be home to Nordstrom's three-level Los Angeles flagship store featuring its latest design concepts, a completely remodeled three-level Bloomingdale's, a brand-new two-level Macy's, as well as the world-renowned Eataly, the largest Italian marketplace in the world.

Twenty new residences across ten floors will also be added, making the Westfield a landmark destination.

Location: Los Angeles, CA
Client: Westfield
Team: Gensler, Kelly Wearstler Design, Selbert Perkins Design, RA Smith National, HLB Lighting Design

GLENDALE 180

Glendale 180 is a 350,000-SF open-air retail, dining, entertainment, and hospitality development that sits on roughly 22 acres in Glendale, Colorado. Just south of Denver and under a mile from the Cherry Creek Shopping District, Glendale 180 creates a unique and new entertainment district that will restore Glendale's reputation as a distinct and dynamic social hub.

Three defining principles are incorporated into the design of Glendale 180 – culture, nature, and leisure. Those principles are woven together to shape and create a cohesive design that establishes flow and encourages social activity.

The project's design, comprised of walkways, plazas, and bridges across several levels, as well as the numerous points of entry, will serve as both gateway and connector, encouraging activity and drawing in pedestrians from the surrounding destinations. Glendale 180 marries neighborhoods, including the shopping district to the north and will feature trails, waterways, cultural sites, nightlife attractions, 25 restaurants, and a centrally located park for people seeking recreation, whether active or passive.

The design intent is reflective of Colorado's iconic landscape and the city's desire to make Glendale an entertainment capital. Cherry Creek and the Rocky Mountains are prominently exposed in the background and are a part of the unique experience at Glendale 180. The architecture and landscape allow for flexible programming for residents and visiting guests while celebrating a few of the local's favorite activities.

Location: Denver, CO
Client: City of Glendale
Team: Gensler, Turner Construction, Martin/Martin Engineers, Kumar & Associates, Taylor and Miller LIGHT, TDA Colorado, Watry Design, Syska Hennesy Group, Square Peg Design

MCKINNEY AND OLIVE

Located at one of the most prominent street sections in Uptown Dallas, McKinney and Olive, will be the tallest building in the district at 22 stories. The planned 530,000-GSF, mixed-use development is designed by Pelli Clarke Pelli Architects. McKinney and Olive makes a bold architectural statement, creating a distinctive address for business and retail.

The project aims to create a pedestrian-friendly environment complete with shopping, restaurants, and other retail all facing on a 36,000-SF piazza. The Piazza will serve as the focus of the development and will include botanical gardens, large mature shade trees, event decks, an activity lawn for special events, a meandering water feature, and numerous places for dining and socialization.

Situated on the fifth floor of the tower, over a portion of the adjacent parking structure, a 5,300-SF Sky Garden is provided as a break-out space for conferencing and workout facilities. This garden includes botanical plantings, shade trees, and seating areas.

Location: Dallas, TX
Client: Crescent Real Estate Equities
Team: Pelli Clarke Pelli Architects, Kendall/Heaton Associates, Brockette Davis Drake,
                I.A. Naman + Associates, Quentin Thomas & Associates

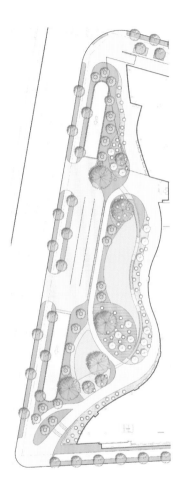

PARK DISTRICT

Sited on a three-acre parcel located between Pearl Street, Olive Street, and Klyde Warren Park, Park District is a new 19-story, 916,000-SF, mixed-use project slated for completion in Q4 2016. The tower will feature Class A offices, luxury residences, ground-floor retail, extensive below-grade parking, and a plaza designed by OJB. Park District Tower will provide tenants with efficient floor plates, multiple outdoor terraces, a state-of-the-art fitness facility, a full conference facility with meeting rooms, and a grand lobby with luxury hotel-like space for informal meetings. In an effort to integrate Park District into the existing fabric of the neighborhood, the vast majority of office, residential, and visitor parking will be located in a below-grade garage to allow relief along Klyde Warren Park. The project's design emphasizes strong connections to Klyde Warren Park with wide, inviting sidewalks, park-like landscaping, and a large, walkable plaza with valet pick-up and drop-off.

Location: Dallas, TX
Owner: Trammell Crow Company
Team: HKS, Brockette Davis Drake, Blum Consulting Engineers, Purdy-McGuire, Halff Associates

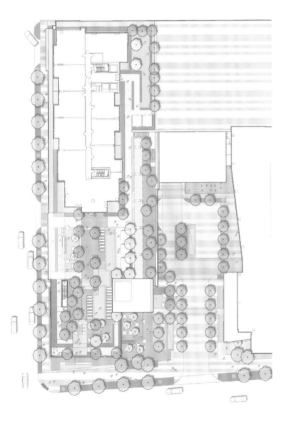

ACADEMIC CAMPUS

ENRICHING EXPERIENCES OUTSIDE OF THE CLASSROOM

As one of the leading designers of academic campuses in the United States, OJB understands the requirements to produce an active, dynamic, and engaging landscape. A network of open spaces of adequate scale and design deliver relief from the built environment while providing human-scale places for socialization, contemplation, and circulation.

OJB's schemes contribute to the existing character of a campus. The designs strengthen the association the students, faculty, and staff have with the institution and its vernacular landscape. Use of regionally specific plant palettes reflects the local ecology and aesthetic while providing a reprieve from the surrounding structures. Proper material selection is crucial to achieving the goal of aesthetic coherence amongst materials. Various typologies in pavements, plantings, and furnishings assist in campus wayfinding and identification of key locations.

A planned geometry of connections contributes to campus circulation and interactions, providing users with an assortment of options for linkages throughout campus.

BROCKMAN HALL FOR PHYSICS AT RICE UNIVERSITY

The Brockman Hall for Physics is an 111,000-SF facility housing classrooms, laboratory space, lecture halls, and administrative offices for the Physics Department as well as physicists from the Electrical and Computer Engineering Department at Rice University in Houston. Driven by Rice University's belief that some of the most important moments on campus are instances of informal discussion and debate outside of the classroom, the design of the building and landscape seeks to provide a multitude of spaces for lively and inspiring conversation.

Sheltered from the sun by the building overhead, a ground-floor courtyard features a reflecting pool, raised ipe terrace, and enhanced plaza with movable furniture. OJB was also asked to redesign the "Courtyard of Science," an interstitial space between the wings of Brown Hall to the south. A grove of honey mesquites organizes the space and intimate decomposed granite courtyards with movable furniture create a number of social spaces.

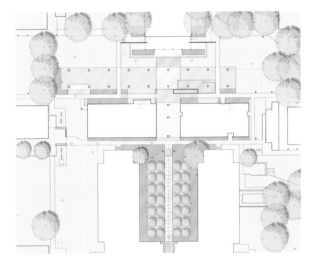

Location: Houston, TX
Client: Rice University
Team: KieranTimberlake, Arup Lighting, Walter P. Moore, Haynes Whaley Associates,
          CCRD Partners, Perkins+Will, JEAcoustics, Ulrich Engineers
Awards: SCUP/AIA-CAE Honor Award, Excellence in Architecture for a New Building
          AIA Houston Design Award

BROCHSTEIN PAVILION AT RICE UNIVERSITY

Developed as a key element of the "Vision for the Second Century" strategic plan, the Brochstein Pavilion has transformed the Central Quadrangle into the social center of the Rice University campus. The 6,000-SF pavilion offers light refreshments and features a 10,000-SF covered outdoor terrace. Set in a field of decomposed granite, a grove of 48 allée lacebark elms responds to the grid of the building and organizes the space between the Pavilion and the adjacent Fondren Library.

Two low concrete fountains define the space under the canopy, and movable seating accommodates impromptu gatherings of students and faculty. Additional plantings of live oaks and improved pedestrian paths reinforce the existing framework of the Quadrangle.

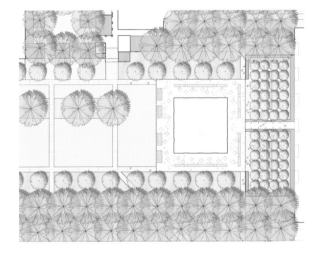

Location: Houston, TX
Client: Rice University
Team: Thomas Phifer & Partners, Fisher Marantz Stone, Walter P. Moore, Ulrich Engineers,
           Altieri Sebor Wieber, Haynes Whaley Associates
Awards: ASLA National Design Award
           ASLA Texas Chapter Merit Award
           AIA National Honor Award
           AS&U Architectural Citation

MCLANE STADIUM AT BAYLOR UNIVERSITY

In Spring of 2012, Baylor University announced that they would retire the 60-year-old off-campus stadium and build a new arena on-campus. The 93-acre site selected for the new stadium sits along the Brazos River. A pedestrian bridge spanning the river connects the stadium site to the university campus. The location of the relocated arena creates a stronger connection to the main campus giving students the opportunity to walk from classrooms and dorms to sporting events and offers visitors a unique game day and tailgating experience.

OJB provided planting and irrigation design for the landscape around the stadium, including planting beds, turf, native grasses, seeded areas, and indigenous plants. The irrigation design reduces water consumption and waste associated with typical irrigation practices for the conservation of natural resources.

OJB introduced a new planting palette, including ornamental grasses and wildflowers, which is atypical of what has been done traditionally at Baylor. The large sweeps of planting were influenced by the curvature of the bridge and the river's edge. This new planting palette, along with the live oak "ring" around the stadium and tailgating areas, distinguishes the stadium side of the campus.

OJB designed the walks and spaces around the stadium, creating better pedestrian circulation and allowing for programmed spaces. A landscaped plaza was designed with trees, ornamental planting, and shaded courtyard areas, to accommodate the high volume of pedestrian traffic during sporting events.

Location: Waco, TX
Client: Baylor University
Team: Populous

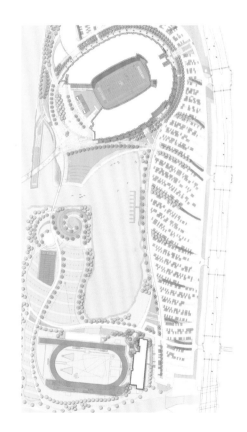

THE ANNENBERG CENTER FOR INFORMATION SCIENCE AND TECHNOLOGY
AT THE CALIFORNIA INSTITUTE OF TECHNOLOGY

The Annenberg Center for Information Science and Technology at the California Institute of Technology provides a modern center for collaborative research and instruction in the disciplines of science and engineering. The facility represents Caltech's sustainability initiatives and is LEED Gold certified. The landscape surrounding the building reflects this environmental ethic and exhibits a substantial departure from the traditional Pasadena ornamental palette.

Palo verde trees structure the building's entry plantings, which are organized into a series of planks to echo the adjacent glass façade. The shrub understory heavily focuses on water conservation and is comprised of a number of succulents and ornamental grasses. The project also includes a significant social component through its provision of decomposed granite seating areas and movable furniture, which are used for casual outdoor gatherings. The new environmental aesthetic, with its concomitant water conservation benefits, is being enthusiastically embraced by the   campus community.

Location: Los Angeles, CA
Client: The Annenberg Center for Information Science and Technology
           at the California Institute of Technology
Team: Frederick Fisher and Partners, HLB Lighting Design, KPFF Consulting Engineers

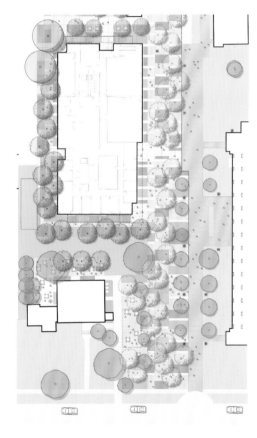

MESA COLLEGE QUADRANGLE MASTER PLAN

The quadrangle master plan for Mesa College in San Diego creates an important new five-acre central open space for one of California's largest junior colleges. Funded by $2B of public bond initiatives, the campus is undergoing a series of significant new building projects that will now be united by a landscape design that responds to local climate and ecology. Working closely with staff from the San Diego Community College District and a broad group of Mesa College stakeholders, OJB conducted a series of campus workshops to define the programming and design of the campus' open spaces. Recommendations from the master plan guide the selection of materials, furnishings, environmental graphics, and landscape elements to ensure continuity between all new campus open spaces.

A central "town square" plaza unites the new Instructional Technology and Cafeteria buildings and provides a central public space for student activity. Embracing the plaza is a 28,000-SF great lawn bounded by gravel courts with shade trees and movable furniture. A new performance pavilion accommodates large campus events and provides a recognizable landmark in the quadrangle. A meandering bioswale buffers the central lawn from classroom spaces, filters stormwater on-site, and showcases a variety of native San Diego plant communities.

OJB is currently collaborating with design/build teams for each building project to ensure the master plan is implemented as originally envisioned.

Location: San Diego, CA
Client: San Diego Community College District

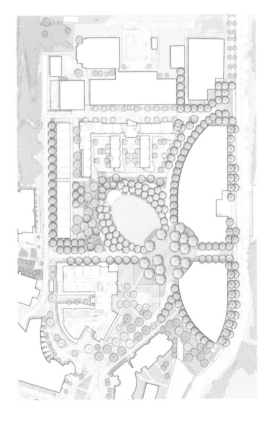

OJB HISTORY & PHILOSOPHY

The Office of James Burnett focuses on creating landscapes that transform perspectives and evoke emotional responses. The firm's work imaginatively unifies the relationship between landscape and architecture, ensuring unique compositions that satisfy the demands of both form and function.

Creating unique and unforgettable sensory experiences that promote healthy living is core to OJB's design ethos. The firm's early work was rooted in healthcare, where Jim Burnett tapped his personal and professional experience to design supportive, healthy, and restorative environments. This careful analysis of landscape's interaction with the senses became a driving force in OJB's designs and has been translated into the firm's work across all verticals – academic, civic, cultural, office, hospitality, mixed-use, and retail.

OJB's design process conceives original and inventive landscapes within the framework of context and function, mitigating site challenges with creative and innovative solutions. The firm is committed to an inclusive, exploratory process that engages and inspires project stakeholders and collaborators; OJB's integrated, multi-disciplinary approach has sustained the relevance of the firm throughout its 27-year history as it continues to challenge the conventional boundaries of landscape architecture.

Jim founded the Office of James Burnett in 1989 in Houston, Texas. The firm's early projects were thoughtful and composed, quickly establishing OJB as a leader in the field of landscape architecture. By 2003, OJB opened a second office in San Diego, CA. The new location expanded OJB's reach to the west coast, and the firm grew quickly. In 2013, OJB opened its Boston office and currently employs 60 professionals throughout the firm.

SELECT HONORS

2016 ASLA Design Medal - James Burnett

2015 ASLA Firm Award - National

2015 Urban Land Institute (ULI) Urban Open Space Award, for Myriad Botanical Gardens, Oklahoma City, Oklahoma

2014 Urban Land Institute (ULI) Urban Open Space Award, for Klyde Warren Park, Dallas, Texas

ASLA National Design Award, for Sunnylands Center & Gardens, Rancho Mirage, California

ASLA Texas Design Award, for Klyde Warren Park, Dallas, Texas

ASLA Texas Design Award, for The Brochstein Pavilion at Rice University, Houston, Texas

Urban Land Institute (ULI) Houston Award of Distinction, for CityCentre Houston, Houston, Texas

ASLA San Diego Design Award, for Sunnylands Center & Gardens, Rancho Mirage, California

ASLA San Diego Design Award, for Annenberg Center for Information Science and Technology at the California Institute of Technology, Pasadena, California

ASLA National Design Award, for The Brochstein Pavilion at Rice University, Houston, Texas

ASLA San Diego Design Award, for Myriad Botanical Gardens, Oklahoma City, Oklahoma

AIA California Award, for Playa Vista Central Park, Playa Vista, California

Burnham Award for Planning Excellence, for The Park at Lakeshore East, Chicago, Illinois

AIA Institute Honor Award, for Regional and Urban Design, for Beijing CBD, Beijing, China

ASLA Texas Design Award, for CityCentre Houston, Houston, Texas

ASLA Texas Planning Award, for Project 180, Oklahoma City, Oklahoma

ASLA Texas Design Award, for ConocoPhillips World Headquarters, Houston, Texas

ASLA Texas Design Award, for Enterprise Plaza at 1100 Louisiana, Houston, Texas

ASLA San Diego Design Award, for La Jolla Commons, La Jolla, CA

The American Architecture Award, The Chicago Athenaeum Museum of Architecture & Design, for The Park at Lakeshore East, Chicago, Illinois

FIABCI Prix 'd Excellence Award, for The Lakeshore East Master Plan, Chicago, Illinois

ASLA Texas Design Award for Beijing Television Station, Beijing, China

Best New Park - Chicago Magazine, for The Park at Lakeshore East, Chicago, Illinois

ASLA Texas Design Award, for The Park at Lakeshore East, Chicago, Illinois

ASLA Texas Design Award, for Waterway 1 & 2 The Woodlands, Texas

ASLA Texas Design Award, for The Crossings, Austin, Texas

AIA Excellence in Regional and Urban Design, for Lakeshore East Master Plan, Chicago, Illinois

ASLA Texas Design Award, for Splitrock Services, Houston, Texas

ASLA Texas Design Award, for Warren Medical Office Building, Tulsa, Oklahoma

ASLA Texas Design Award, for Exxon Greens Road Campus, Houston, Texas

ASLA Texas Design Award, for Introgen Therapeutics, Houston, Texas

ASLA Texas Design Award, for Westwood Technology Center, Houston, Texas

ASLA National Design Award, for Reid Residence, Houston, Texas

ASLA Texas Design Award, for The Enclave, Office Complex, Houston, Texas

ASLA Texas Design Award, for Reid Residence, Houston, Texas

ASLA Texas Design Award, for Exxon Production & Research Facility, Houston, Texas

Tucker Design Award - The Building Stone Institute, for The Park at Lakeshore East, Chicago, Illinois

ASLA Texas Design Award, for NASA Astronaut Quarantine Facility, Clear Lake, Texas

ASLA Texas Design Award, for 9/11 Memorial, Houston, Texas

ASLA Texas Design Award, for Halliburton Plaza at Minute Maid Park, Houston, Texas

ASLA Texas Design Award, for Polk Street Substation, Houston, Texas

ASLA Texas Design Award, for Malkhassian Residence, Houston, Texas

ASLA Texas Design Award, for First Presbyterian Church Memorial Garden, Houston, Texas

Excellence in Marketing & Communications - Landscape Architecture Magazine, National Award, multiple awards

ASLA Texas Design Award, for Memorial Hermann HBU Wellness Center, Houston, Texas

ASLA Texas Planning Award, for Exxon Brookhollow Campus Master Plan, Houston, Texas

ASLA Texas Design Award, for Methodist Community Health Center, Sugar Land, Texas

ASLA Texas Design Award, for American General Call Center, Houston, Texas

ASLA Texas Design Award, for Central Michigan University, Sculpture Court

ASLA Texas Design Award, for Haskell Street Townhomes, Houston, Texas

ASLA Texas Design Award, for St. Elizabeth Hospital, Hebert Health & Wellness Center, Beaumont, Texas

ASLA Texas Design Award, for Exxon Brookhollow Heart of the Campus, Houston, Texas

ASLA Texas Design Award, for St. Michael Rehabilitation Hospital, Texarkana, Texas

ASLA Texas Design Award, for Airport Community Farms

ASLA Texas Design Award, for St. Elizabeth Hospital Master Plan, Beaumont, Texas

I.D. Annual Design Review, Honorable Mention, for Airport Community Farms

LEADERSHIP

James Burnett, President
Chip Trageser, Partner
Jereck Boss, Partner
Meg Levy, Chief Operations Officer

Dillon Diers, Principal
Nathan Elliott, Principal
Kyle Fiddelke, Principal
Cody Klein, Principal

Andrew Albers, Vice President
Claudia Thome, Director of Operations

TEAM

Simon Beer
Brittany Blicharz
Scott Blons
Tarah Brand
Ben Canales
Charlie Cattlett
Andrew Cridlin
Adrianne Cruz
Lisa Davis
Cynthia Dehlavi
Erin Dibos
Brian Dickson
J. Ryan Harbert
Ryan Harrison

Sam Heritage
Kim Hurlock
Tyler Jurney
Judy Lee Shern
Caroline Lezon
Victoria Lorenz
Cheryl Lough
Nabyl Macias
Maria Mateo-Castro
Rebecca McKevitz
Andrew Miller
Alexander Nagel
Katie Nguyen
Jamin Pablo

Charlie Palanza
Shi Park
Sean Passler
Lana Peralta
Chris Shern
Sookyung Shin
Rachel Sloan
Drew Stangel
Ryan Steib
Cindy Tong
Troy Vaughn
Allison Walling
Linda West
Rachel Wilkins

IMAGE CREDITS

Aerial Photography Inc	10
Andrew Miller	147
Blake Marvin	136, 138, 140, 141
Carl Shortt	24, 26, 27
Chip Trageser	146
Christy Radecic	198, 200, 201, 202, 203
Cody Klein	130, 131, 132, 133
Dallas News	22
David Cobb	28, 30, 36, 37, 48, 50
Dillon Diers Photography	15, 16, 17, 44, 47, 66, 70, 74, 75, 79, 80, 82, 102, 108, 110
Fluidity Design Consultants	8
Gary Zvonkovic	19
Hester + Hardaway	38, 40, 41, 42, 86, 87, 90, 92, 93, 94, 95, 96, 97, 98, 99, 100, 101, 115, 125, 134, 135, 190, 192, 194, 196, 197, 208
HKS (renderings)	188
Jeff Fantich, Asia Society Texas	84
Jereck Boss	51
Joshua Spitzig	20
Ken Hayden	71
Liane Swanson Photography	14, 21
Limelife	104, 105, 106, 107, 109
Marion Brenner	15, 16, 18, 23, 28, 34, 35, 45, 46, 47, 72, 73, 76, 88, 112, 113, 114, 116, 118, 120, 121, 124, 126, 127, 142, 144, 145
Matt McKinney	148, 150, 151
Mei-Chun Jau	16
Midway Companies	156, 164
NeoScape (renderings)	158, 160, 161, 162, 163
Prakash Patel	29, 32
Ryan Gobuty	92, 93
Simon Hurst	122
Steinkamp Photography	38, 39, 40
Sybille Allgaier	68, 71, 78, 83
Thomas McConnell	12
Tom Rossiter	152, 154, 155
Zach Nash	31